21-Days to the Love of Your Life

by kac young

Design and typesetting by
John Cole GRAPHIC DESIGNER, Santa Fe, New Mexico

ISBN: 0-9779431-2-7

SAN number: 850-6876

FIRST PRINTING April 2006

This book is dedicated to

The Love of My Life
and
all of the cats who put up with me until I
found it!

SPECIAL THANK YOUS

AND

ACKNOWLEDGEMENTS

Charlie O'Donnell
Ellen Lerner O'Donnell
Peggy and Danny Jones
Jerry Luedders
Tonya Andrews
Carole Tashel, my beloved and patient
    editor,
John Cole, my brilliant graphic designer
Marlene Morris, the one who does
    everything else.

And Felines:
Summer
Lucy
Dot
Zain
and
my beloved Jabez

TABLE OF CONTENTS

Over the years I have found that friends are either delighted for you in your new relationship, or they are jealous. The ones who already have great relationships are happy. For the most part those who don't are usually happy for you at first; but then that little green monster of envy creeps in, especially when you are no longer available for movies and singles events and they become envious and jealous of your new love.

I can't blame them. I was probably the same way between relationships. But now, I have the solution. Since I have stepped into my fabulous fifties, I have this overwhelming urge to share what I know. I have shared my 21-Day Process with several friends over the years and have watched them create wonderful relationships with the information. Since I'm not able to meet with absolutely everyone in the world who wants to find a mate, I decided to write it all down in an easy to-follow-guide so everyone, everywhere can find the right person with whom to share his or her life.

From this point on, there need be no more jealousy. Open the book, read the words, do the exercises and watch what happens! This book will change your life. You'll want to have extra copies of it on hand. Once you do the process and attract *The Love of Your Life* you'll want to prevent any jealousy by handing your single friends this book. It will keep them busy for 21 days, and you'll be doing them a wonderful service.

It is my great pleasure to pass this process along to men and women who are searching for their soul mate, heartthrob, life mate and partner. So to all you lovers and wanna-be spouses out there, take hold of this process and get started today.

Let's take the wedding business by storm!

CHAPTER ONE

Happy Endings Have to Start Somewhere

When I was forty years old I fit the profile of an unmarried "older woman" perfectly. Sure, my clock was ticking but I was successful in business and a fun-loving, yoga practicing, high achiever, with lots of friends, a comfortable life, a disposable income and *thoroughly unsatisfied in love and romance.* I had a great job, a career of which I was enormously proud, a plethora of certificates on the wall, a lovely home, a full social calendar, a passport full of stamps from foreign countries, an accumulation of airline miles, designer handbags from New York City, and a palm pilot with enough plans and activities to fill the next five years. There was never a dull moment in my life, yet I was still seeking the one thing I lacked: a real and true romantic relationship with *The Love of My Life.*

Like many other women my age I had dated, fallen in love, had my heart broken and was actually engaged once (until his wife stepped in and called it off). Then one day, I ran into an old friend in the coffee shop of what used to be the old Schwab's Drug Store in Beverly Hills. I was in the building for a consultation on some "youthening facial procedures" and he was visiting his new girlfriend, soon to become wife, who worked in the office of the same "youth" doctor whom I was visiting. Quite a nice coincidence. We sat down with some coffee to chat and catch up.

I had known this gentleman for thirty years. He is one of Hollywood's top announcers (you know, the voice you hear announcing all the stars' names on the award shows or the prizes on the game shows). He and I had worked on many, many television shows together. He was always smiling, happy and gregarious. He also had been happily married for a zillion years until his wife died. He confided to me that he stayed very busy for quite a few years to divert himself from the pain of her loss and to cover up the loneliness he felt. But he had recovered. And then he began to tell me his story of falling in love. He couldn't wait to reveal the secrets of how he created a direct line to finding *The Love of His Life.*

His story went something like this: After almost four years of being alone and then having an unrewarding date here and there, he felt hollow. At this point a friend introduced him to the world of spirituality and metaphysics. He was captivated by the new ideas. While visiting a New Thought bookstore his interest was piqued by a book on affirmations. After reading the book he decided to attempt a process of 21 days of written declarations and affirmations. The book suggested he be completely honest in describing the kind of mate he was seeking. He realized it was not necessarily an easy-breezy task, but he was determined to do the work and he made a commitment to finish one legal page each night.

At first the work went well and he easily used up two or three pages describing the person with whom he wanted to share his life. But by the fifth and sixth night it became a lot harder to find new ways to say what was on his mind. It was starting to take him an average of two to three hours a night to fill a page. Yet he wanted someone he could love and cherish, so he persisted in his effort to precisely and meticulously describe the fabulous partner he desired. At the end of the 21days he proofread his work. When he was satisfied with each and every one of the affirmations, details and descriptions, he went into his back yard and lit all the pages on fire. Ceremoniously, he sent the smoke from the burning pages out into the universe so those cosmic energies could respond to his statements. Thirty days later a magnificent woman came into his life. She was *exactly* what he had described. This process attracted his dream woman into his life. Four months later they were engaged, and five months after that they were married.

I listened attentively to his love story and to the details of the search that brought him into the world of sparkling eyes, animated speech, and the kind of dynamic energy that only lovers in love seem to have. I was captivated by his story and consumed with happiness for this man with whom I had shared so many years of a working friendship. It didn't occur to me until much later that what he did to find true love could work a second time. Or, that his winning process could actually be duplicated by someone like me, too.

When it finally hit me, I did a ton of soul

searching. Was I really ready for this? I had to take stock. I had to answer a lot of really hard questions before I embarked on this love cruise. If this process really worked, was I really and truly ready for the results? Did I want a real mate, or did I just want company? Was I truly willing to share my life, or did I just need a handy-man? Could I love myself enough by myself, or was I expecting someone else to fill in those blanks for me? Did I know enough about relationships to have one that lasted a lifetime? When I felt I had asked and answered all of these questions, I put my friend's plan to work.

I was astounded at the results. (Imagine now you are hearing a church organ play, *Here Comes the Bride*. It makes the point!) I was so successful that many of my friends asked me to teach them the process. And so I did. Their successes begat other successes until finally I decided to let everyone in on the secret and write this book. Why shouldn't anyone and everyone who wants to have a mate have one? Why shouldn't we all find the *Loves of Our Lives*? We can. I did, twice!

If you are willing to commit the next 21 consecutive days to this process, you too can easily become one of the success stories.

There's an old Italian saying which is on a plaque that hangs in my dining room. It says: *Vive bene, spesso l'amore, di risata molto.* If you prefer it in French, *Habiter bien, l'amour beaucoup de et rire souvent;* or perhaps if you're Dutch, *Leef wens, hou van veel, lach dikwijls.*

The English translation is simply, *Live well, love much and laugh often.*

I wish you all of that and more!

CHAPTER TWO

My Own Story

There have been five *Loves of My Life*. The first was a lad named Danny. He was a serious and powerful crush in the ninth grade. He was student body president; I was class president. He was captain of the football team; I was head cheerleader. We were mad for each other. Our ninth grade year was filled with touchdowns, pom poms, first kisses, late night forbidden phone calls, clandestine love notes passed in class, and finally the news of my acceptance into private school 100 miles away. I say *finally* because, like a hot coal, Danny dropped me. He said he couldn't go on with a relationship that was doomed to end when I left for school. I was devastated. He broke up with me in June. That left the whole summer to be depressed and to navigate my social and emotional life all alone. I blamed my parents; I blamed everyone. It just wasn't *fair*. In my fantasy, although I would be gone during the school week, I could see Danny on weekends and I would still be able to attend all of his high school football games and certainly all of the parties. He didn't see it that way. Or perhaps he was looking for a way out. I'll never know. I just know I was crushed and spent the summer moping around feeling unloved, dejected and abandoned. *Poor me!*

We did get together one more time when he took me to my college prom, but by then most of his feelings had diminished, and I was the only one holding a match-sized flame. He moved on to police work, marriage and a family and I moved on too.

The next *Love of My Life* was actually an account executive for the company sponsoring the television shows I was producing. He was bright, hilariously funny and always meddling in what I considered to be my creative business. He grew on me. We had heated rows which were always emotionally charged but respectful, exciting and in retrospect quite healthy and creative. When we weren't talking work, he related how unhappy he was in his marriage. He felt his wife didn't appreciate him or all the hours he worked to support her and their child. She nagged him constantly to lose weight and didn't truly support his career goals beyond his current job. Both of us were very clear that our relationship was professional and if personal at all, a nice friendship.

Until one fateful night. We were on deadline for some scripts and he was hounding me for the revisions, which I didn't have. I was dog-tired, I couldn't have read them even if they were on my desk. The writers were writing as fast as they could and we just could not do anything faster. We had words; his demanding and mine shrill and over the edge. This was not a smart thing to do on my part since he "okayed" the payment check written by his company to my company.

I decided to take a rest for a few minutes since there was nothing I could do but hope and trust: we were shooting eleven half-hour shows in the morning and I only had scripts for seven. Sitting in my backyard in the hot tub, about as tired and nervous as any person could be, I was sipping on a glass of white wine as he came around the corner of my backyard fence and jumped into the hot tub fully clothed! That certainly broke the tension and we laughed and laughed. What's a girl to do? I couldn't let him go home in his wet Brooks

Brothers suit. One thing led to another, and let's just say there weren't any further discussions about the missing scripts until morning.

We talked endlessly about his failing marriage and we talked about the meaning of our night together. We talked and talked and talked. After the shoot, which lasted a couple of weeks, he had to go home either to face the music or create a new song. We spent an incredible weekend in the Walter Winchell bungalow at the Ambassador Hotel (home of the Mrs. Robinson bar from the movie *The Graduate*). We managed a tearful goodbye as he headed for the airport and the east coast. I mustered the courage to say to him (though I probably only believed fifty-one percent of it to be true) that I hoped he would go back and do whatever was necessary to work out his marriage. He wouldn't be the man I knew him to be if he left a possibility unexplored. I only wanted him when he was completely *sure* the marriage was over and he absolutely knew he wanted out. (And that's exactly what I told myself to believe over and over.) The plan we made together was for him to write his letter of resignation from his V.P. position on Madison Avenue on the plane, then tell his wife he wanted a divorce and would be moving to the west coast. It was April 10th and he was scheduled, if everything went like the movies tell you it will, to be back in LA for good with me on June 6th. One hour after he left, 100 roses were delivered to my door. When I opened the card to see who they were from, the card simply read, "You had to look?"

The next few weeks were glorious. I was totally enthralled with recreating the house to fit him in. I didn't call or write because I knew he was dealing with a lot of difficult things. He had rehearsed his farewell speech over and over with me and I had no reason to doubt he would deliver it.

However, 3000 miles away on the east coast, the wife, hearing of his unfaithfulness and intention to move away, flew into a rage. She taunted him with everything she could think of that might intimidate or terrify him. The worst blow being the threat he would never see his child again. He quivered and quaked and then he agreed to go into couple's counseling to save the marriage. He called a few times to tell me what was going on in the counseling sessions. I listened as many times as I could, and then I knew I needed to set him free. If he wanted to attempt to mend his marriage, he needed to have my full support and blessing; otherwise I would be "the other woman" and a home-wrecker for the rest of our lives together.

In counseling, his wife let him have it and stirred up every bit of guilt and blame she could. She weakened his resolve with her words and ultimately her actions. He was stuck. Instead of arriving in LA on June 6th, he called me to announce his wife was pregnant with their second child. After he hung up, I called the airport, bought a ticket, hailed a taxi, boarded a plane and went to Greece. I sobbed all the way to Athens, and all the way to Delphi, and all the way to Myconos and all the way to Thessalonica. After 6,000 miles of crying I finally dried up and got hold of myself.

Then my life got even worse. Upon my return I was faced with the cancellation of three of my television shows and the subsequent need to "fire" everyone in my company since we had no product to produce. I had to "let go" twelve regular employees and twenty part timers. For about a week I just took to my bed. I ate bagels and Milk Duds for six days straight and then on the seventh day, I got up and did what I had to do. For some reason The Fates had decided to put me to work and my sorrows and disappointments (mostly at myself for being such a gullible jug head) were drowned in sixteen-hour television production days. I worked straight with no vacations for the next three years. My work took me to the east coast and I did see the ex-Love a few times (mostly to drop off another baby present and another and another). Before it was over, the wife had three more children and put him in debt for the rest of his life. By the way, she ended up cheating on him "to get even" and they have been divorced for eighteen years. I am not one bit gleeful, only sad for him. He was a good guy, once upon a time.

But back to my story: When I got back from Greece and scrubbed my tear-stained face with Comet, I drove myself to a consultation with a leading Beverly Hills surgeon. I thought having a smaller (Barbie-like) waist would solve all my relationship problems, or at least rectify the effects of the bagels and Milk Duds. I don't know what I was thinking, but it was a distraction of some sort. I underwent liposuction for my middle and then busied myself by being the *surgery express*, escorting various other friends to and from the plastic surgeon. We all spent the summer looking for the secret of youth under the knife. All in all, it was fairly entertaining. Every one of my close friends was sucked, wrapped and bruised, by choice, between July and August. We passed tubes of holistic Arnica cream back and forth like a Frisbee.

Three years of furious and exciting work followed this heartshaker. I underwent some "art therapy" (this counselor had a degree in art plus psychology so clients don't have to say "shrink") to figure out why I kept attracting the "unavailable" types. I adopted a couple of really swell cats and focused my attention on them and my work. They were wonderful to come home to after a long day at the studio, so I was content for a while with purring faces, litter boxes and Friskies between *The Loves of My Life.*

Some people find dates by being intro-duced by friends, others look on the Internet. Some find activities and clubs to join and some just frequent to bars. I accidentally discovered a new and different way to meet men. I got run over by my own car. It was a simple workday morning and my Mercedes wouldn't start, again. It had been having ignition prob-lems, but every time I took it to Hans at the shop, it worked perfectly. Typical. This partic-ular morning it refused to start and Hans had told me to call the minute it happened again and have it towed to him immediately. Maybe he could isolate the problem if he could find it right away. So I did just that.

The towing company responded right away and the repair garage was right across the street from my office, so not too much time would be lost in the process. Sweet. Only one problem. The tow truck driver was a little hung-over from his celebrations at a bachelor party the night before. He rubbed his forehead while asking me if I had any rope to tie off the steering wheel. A Mercedes is towed from the back to preserve its renowned German alignment, so he needed to immobilize the steering wheel from turning in transit. I didn't have any rope handy, but offered him a scrawny little piece of twine from the Sunday paper that was lying on the garage floor. He was thrilled and used the plastic twine to tie off the wheel. Little did I know this was one of the stupidest things ever done in the chronicles of car-towing adventures.

Leaving the house, we rounded the first corner and immediately "snap!" went the twine. Then the tow truck lurched forward from the force of the Mercedes careening out into the street and coincidently sideswiping an innocently parked truck. Then "whack!"

another lurch and the still-attached Mercedes careened into *another* car. My car was gleefully swinging back and forth across the street behind the tow truck, like a tennis ball on a bungee cord, wreaking havoc on anything and everything except one wise and quick-footed pedestrian who nimbly dodged the auto-gone-berserk. I watched in horror as the "towing guy" jumped out of the cab like he was going to "catch" the car with his hands and stop it from bludgeoning innocent vehicles. Adding to the now surreal incident, I suddenly became aware that the tow truck had lurched out of gear and was headed down the street obviously with a mind of its own, me in it and no driver.

There was a huge pile of clipboards, rags and assorted towing and unidentifiable paraphernalia between the driver's side and me. I knew I couldn't reach the brakes in time, and all I could see ahead of me was a very tall, thick palm tree and a house. Clearly, nothing good could possibly come of this, so I did what any brave viewer of *Extreme Sports* would do: I jumped out of the cab and landed face-down on the pavement. At the same time, the Mercedes lurched once again and headed back over to where I was lying (after whamming yet another parked car). My faithful car ran straight over the tops of my legs twisting me into a pretzel and tossing me unceremoniously into a neighbor's yard. Plunk and splat, there I was.

I had never met the neighbor before, Doctor Cheung, but he was just coming home from working the night shift at St. Joseph's hospital. He was quite surprised to find me in his front yard, along with a now badly dented Mercedes which was tied to a tow truck at the end of the road, and accordioned into a palm tree, steaming like a cartoon. The lone voice in the midst of this dramatic moment was that of the tow truck driver. He was standing in the middle of the street wringing his hands, rubbing his head and muttering over and over, "My wife is going to kill me." All I could think of was, " Tell her to take a ticket and get in line! Hello? Some of us are injured here, pal!!!!! Can you at least call 911 or something?" Gratefully, Dr. Cheung called ahead to the admitting room of the hospital where I was subsequently taken. Meanwhile, Hans at the Mercedes repair shop was extremely surprised to see a deformed and mangled Mercedes arrive when all he was expecting was an engine that wouldn't start. Delivered to his repair shop was a vehicle that looked strangely like it had already visited the wrecking yard. It took a few conversations and some rusty English-to-German translation to convey to him fully what had happened.

Three weeks I lay in my bed. For three weeks I watched the visible tire tracks on my legs turn every color of the rainbow. For three weeks my front door remained unlocked since I was unable to get up and answer it. Friends, and friends of friends, paraded through my house bringing food and sporting cameras to photograph the, now-becoming-famous legs that featured designer tread marks. All my friends wanted a photo for *their* scrapbook! I felt like the freak stop on the Celebrity Homes Tour.

How this situation became a multiple dating opportunity is almost unreal. I suppose the sheer novelty of my story opened hearts, and there was, after all, a car involved. I was treated to Chinese food almost every night by a well-wishing guy or two. Most of whom delighted in advising me about the finer points of foreign car towing mechanics. Without a doubt I was the local attraction, like the two headed-lady at the circus. I was certainly closer in driving distance to their offices than the LA Zoo. Men dropped by in droves. As painful as it was to move, I made sure I put on makeup by six o'clock every night to greet my callers. They could look at my swollen, pathetic, tread-marked legs, but I wouldn't dare let them see me without eyeliner and mascara.

As a side note, one girlfriend, who lived forty miles away, brought her young daughter all the way over to my house so that she could rip off my covers to reveal my bruised and tattered appendages and cry out, "See Molly, this is why mommy wants you to hold her hand when you cross the street!" I didn't mind. It was all for a good cause. She brought fresh bagels.

So the men came, they visited, they advised, they sympathized and they got to eat Chinese food while they watched the news and got credit for a Boy Scout's good deed. It was kind of fun and helped me heal. I never knew which Gentleman Caller might pop in or what kind of take-out I'd have each night for dinner. Most of them were even kind enough to take out the garbage.

As healing progressed and things got better, my "Gentlemen Caller" visits were reduced to insurance claims adjusters. Those glorious days of bed-ridden dating came to a crushing close. Back on my feet again, after a good six months of recovery, I ventured out into the world with a strong heart, a cane and a couple of wobbly knees.

During this time of bed-ridden recovery I reconnected with a woman I'd done a television series with a few years prior. At the same time as my "car accident" she had a "gate accident." She was simply rolling back the 5,000-pound gate her security-conscious, policeman husband had installed, so she could get to the grocery store for vital vittles. Danny, her husband, had a six-foot tall wrought iron fence installed around their humongous property. It came with a twenty-foot by six-foot iron gate that rolled back and forth on tracks. It was automated, but on this particular day, the motor was having an off day, so my friend Peggy shoved it aside manually. The gate was heavy enough to keep marauding Visigoths out of her yard, but she didn't quite notice that her foot was resting on the track until with one big "whoosh," she sent the gate sliding down it's track and right over her foot. She limped into the house where her son shrieked at the sight of her mangled foot and called Danny, who came home immediately and raced her to the hospital.

She was in her bed in Washington State and I was in mine in Los Angeles. We got into the lovely habit of talking daily to take our minds off our similar situations. At first we compared pain killers and their effects: "Gee, how's that Tylox working out for you today?" "Okie dokie, how's the Vicodin going?" We talked and talked and became really solid friends, bonding because we spent hours and hours and days upon days learning about each other. She had three children and was married at nineteen to a guy who still made her middle-aged pulse race at the mere sight of him walking up the front path. She was actually the white picket fence type, but her husband was a wrought iron security gate kind of guy, so he won the fence design issue when it came right down to it. The more we talked, the more I learned about relationships and how they worked.

From this time forward, she became my stalwart partner and guide in every relationship I ventured into. It was from her experience and her kind heart that I learned what it takes to fall in love, remain loving and stay in love no matter what challenges you face. The key she said, is in selecting the right partner with whom you wish to navigate the journey. She imparted many words of wisdom because she had learned innumerable lessons from the experience of constantly working at her marriage to make it a safe harbor. The only thing she couldn't tell me was how to actually *get* a guy in your mid-thirties. She'd been married for about 350 years by now to a guy she fell in love with in her late teens. She had no idea what it was like "out here." She was snuggled in her cozy, happy home, and I was still out in the big pond swimming with sharks.

The next Love Story was so deeply disgusting and clandestinely disguised that I'm almost hesitant to reveal it. But I will, because I think many of us have one of "these" in our history. He wasn't an alcoholic, but he should have been. He would have been easier to recognize as trouble. Instead, he seemed to be a vulnerable, sweet, trustworthy, considerate guy who just loved to talk endlessly about himself and then when he saw your eyes glaze over, he would switch the topic to *you* and bowl you over with his charm, his memory of your likes and dislikes, his insights and his spells. Oh, he was good. Better than good, he was remarkable at this game. Many saw through him right away, but I didn't. I fell hook, line and sinker for his dreamy blue eyes and his apparently soft, squishy center.

This was another workplace romance. He was absolutely single and just seemed to worship the ground I walked on. Except he really didn't. It was all an act. After he had won my affection and my emotional devotion, he made fun of that behind my back. Now, if you've ever had the feeling people were talking about you when you left the room, this was exactly that uncomfortable, almost slimy, feeling. He was a master at emotional fly-fishing and he had caught not only me, but several others on his hook at the same time. He smoked a lot of pot, I found out later, and he gambled. He referred to himself as "Machi-avellian," but I jokingly tossed this comment aside thinking of him more as a Prince Charming than a demon. Fortunately our relationship never got to the physical point. That was the only thing that saved me from leaping off a tall building once I discovered some fairly creepy details about an incident between him and a waitress during a business trip we both took to Nashville.

The worst experience of all was when my best friend Peggy flew into town for my fortieth birthday party. I had rented a beau-tiful restaurant high in the hills of Topanga

Canyon and invited forty of my most cherished friends. Prince Charming/Machiavelli was there. Peggy noticed a few things about him and brought them to my attention in the morning following the party. I had been able to gloss over a few salient points but she saw them clearly and pointed them out. Unfortunately, this relationship of mine cost her a pretty penny. I had promised to bring him up to visit her and meet Danny. The show we were doing together was scheduled to travel to the Pacific Northwest and Peggy's home-town was on the calendar. She had gotten rid of much of her old furniture that summer and was planning on slowly replacing the major pieces over the next year or two. When she learned of our impending visit to her city, she panicked and immediately went out shopping and ordered a whole new living room full of furniture. She didn't want him to come into a place that wasn't perfect, since she believed in my fantasy about having him as my mate for the rest of my life. She wanted it perfect. So, she spent a few thousand dollars on décor before the birthday party happened. Peggy had met him before and was taken in at first by his suave charm. The night of my fortieth birthday she saw other traits and although it broke her heart to tell me, she did. Fortunately, my self esteem and mental health were stronger by now, so I simply fell into Peggy's arms, and after a bottle of consoling Cabernet, resigned the next day from the highest paying job of my life in order to save my dignity, my soul and my mind. She still has the new furniture and monthly payments.

It was time to call the "youthening expert" once again for a surgical fix. And that was the day I ran into my friend Charlie in the coffee shop. He told me about the 21-Day Process. He described it as his ticket to *Love* and recalled how, just 30 short days to the day after finishing it, he met his wife to be. She was a stunning red-head, tall, fair-skinned, witty, dry, funny as heck, and full of life. Her world was an adorable suburban home, which she owned, a job she loved, a parrot and movies on the weekend with girl-friends. She dated, but no one in particular rang her chimes. One fine day, she was invited to attend an award show and Charlie was the announcer. She walked in, he looked up, his script fell to the floor and he felt his lips go numb as she was introduced to him. By the end of the evening he had asked her out. It was a very fast romance. Other than being hospitalized once due to bites from a jealous parrot, their life has been love-packed ever since. They celebrate their 18th wedding anniversary this year.

They both became dear friends and role models. She was a kick and a half and I couldn't have been happier for both of them. This time I didn't hire the surgeon; I went home and concentrated on the 21-Day Process just as Charlie had explained it to me.

To give you a time frame here, I left my job on September 9th. I had coffee with Charlie on September 13th and I inadvertently met the next *Love of My Life* on September 16th. He was dating a friend of mine, so the meeting was purely a "Hello, how do you do" kind of thing. I began the 21-Day program on October 1st.

Night after night I faithfully wrote down the details and descriptions of *The Love of My Life*. I played soothing music, I let the cats brush against my legs and comfort me. I indulged my ego and my fantasies and spoke every truth I could find to speak in writing. I just let it all flow. During the process my emotions welled-up inside of me and I laughed, and cried, and hurt all over again at the memory of past loves; I also reddened with embarrassment and almost hurled at recalling some "lesser" moments. It was one of the most cleansing and healing processes I ever engaged in. I was reading a lot about "forgiveness" at the time, but I realized that for me, I couldn't forgive anyone anything until I came to terms with what forgiveness meant to me first. Forgiveness was a far cry from what I wanted to do to a few of them! However, I did learn to forgive and I now believe this is a major factor in attracting your true love. Personally, it wasn't an issue of *accepting* what past loves had done (or not done) to me, or *blaming* them for what I perceived they had or hadn't done. It was clearly all about accepting the past as just that: passed, gone, over, history, done, kaput. When I got myself to the emotional place of not desiring revenge or retribution for what I felt I didn't receive from any of my past loves, I was free to seek what I truly wanted and to allow myself the chance to have it. Sour grapes have no place in this process. After all, they didn't *mean* to do any harm, except for maybe Prince Machiavelli, so why should I hold onto anything negative? I released it all and got on with my life. I'll bet there are others out there who had to "release and forgive me" too, so it all balances out in the long run.

My friend Peggy was with me all the way. She wanted me to have a mate as wonderful as her husband, Danny, and she loved that I was working hard to attract the "right" kind of guy. I knew it was important to be specific to avoid ending up with someone incompatible for the long haul. So I wrote and wrote and wrote. It became *the* thing I looked forward to every day. I gave up dinners and movies and all kinds of social invitations to allow time and mental space for this process. It had become so important to me that I didn't want to let anything come between me and my future. So, I worked by day and then wrote by night. Those writing sessions sculpted a completely new reality for me.

I finished my 21-Day commitment on October 21st. Of course, I expected to meet *The Love of My Life* on the 22nd. But I was spared that crushing disappointment by having to go out of town. Work rescued me again. I found myself in Milan at the International Film Market, MIFED. Peggy sent me off with a fond long-distance farewell saying she just knew everything was going to be all right.

And it was more than all right. Milan was an eye-opening experience. Suddenly I was attracting loads of men. I was asked out to dinner, I was kissed in the shadows and I was even proposed to after my "intended" consumed nine martinis. Fortunately, I knew this was "the road" and that nothing ever promised "out there" came true once everyone was back home. But it was exhilarating. I felt "youthened" without the knife and I was bubbling, exuberant and ready to take on life and love again. It was working!

What I hadn't realized was that in doing this 21-Day Process, I had actually "forgiven" the past: (quite unintentionally, at least at the conscious level), I had released any ties that bound me to my previous experiences and was filled with the positive new energy of today. It was a vibrant and vital change and I woke up every morning excited about what the new day might bring.

And so, on November 9, five days after my return from Milan, I met *The* next *Love of My Life*. Previously, I had been introduced to him as her "Mr. Right Now" by my girlfriend, the waitress. She had "borrowed" him from another girlfriend, so in her mind he was just a casual bed buddy. They worked together in the same restaurant. I had no intention of anything other than doing her a favor when she asked me to read his script and I agreed. Now, one of the hazards of being in show biz, no matter what part of it you're actually in, is that people are always asking you to read their scripts. Generally, the writer doesn't actually *care* about your "input" he/she just wants to hear your praise or make use of your connections. It's writer-human nature.

This case was different. Her boyfriend/wannabe-screenwriter actually *was* interested in my thoughts. His script had potential and it dealt with a volatile subject. My notes were simple, direct and clear and he took them in like a thirsty camel. He thanked me for my time and offered to treat me to dinner to repay me for my efforts. He was so gracious. I was touched by his kindness and consideration. There wasn't anything more to it than that. I called Peggy right away and told her all about him. She thought he sounded really nice and wanted to know more.

My girlfriend called the next day and thanked me for reading his script. She said he was excited and was making the revisions I suggested as we spoke. I was thrilled to have made someone's life a little happier. Then he called. He wanted to drop off the changes to see what I thought. I said I would read them when I got a chance. He left them at my door. A few weeks passed, I read the changes and made a couple of notes and dropped the revisions off at the restaurant where he worked. Then he called again. He wanted to take me to dinner and tell me about a celebrity who was reading his script. I phoned my girlfriend to tell her of the invite and she asked me to please go ahead. I did. We had a marvelous time. He tried to give me a little good night kiss, but I dodged it.

He called again and invited me to a concert. I called my girlfriend and she encouraged me to go because he had already asked her and she couldn't attend. I went. We had a great time and this time he hinted at wanting more. I couldn't have been clearer about my stand with regard to him and my girlfriend. I valued and honored my friendship with her and I wasn't going to play around with it. As long as my girlfriend was in his life, he needed to be with her. I had learned that lesson. I wasn't going to consider anything with any man unless he was free, mentally and emotionally available and desirous of an exclusive relationship.

I was so proud at how far I had come and of my newly found wisdom. No more married men for me! Even if they said they were "separated" or "unhappy." No more mischievous, calculating manipulators. No more little boys. I had written my 21-Day testimonial for what and whom I wanted to attract and I was sticking to it, by golly gosh and gee.

My girlfriend called back and while she thanked me for my concern about her relationship with this man, she wanted me to know she wasn't interested in an "exclusive" one with him. In fact, she suggested we "share him," and then she had to hang up because another boyfriend was ringing her doorbell. Being an only child, I didn't know how to share. The closest thing I ever came to share was actually working on the "Cher" variety show for CBS.

He called again. We talked about the conversation with my girlfriend and he confirmed they were not exclusive. He added that he was, in fact, seeing several other women at the same time. Hah! I had just saved myself a huge heartbreak, disappointment and another chance to fail at a relationship. I certainly didn't want a cad. So I just laughed and told him if he was ever *really* free, to give me a call, as I wasn't interested in being "Tuesday" on his weekly list of dates.

Less than two weeks later, he called to say he wanted to meet. He had something important to tell me. He dropped by for a glass of wine and brought with him a steaming skillet of marinara sauce and a handful of uncooked spaghetti, asking as he walked through the door, if I'd mind putting on a pot of water. Flabbergasted, I went to the kitchen, hauled out the kettle and boiled some water. While the sauce was simmering and the pasta was cooking he told me that he'd had a "meeting" with all of his "dates" and told them it was over. Some cried; some were mildly disappointed. He said he'd done this so he could be "free" to date me, exclusively. Second flabbergast for the evening. Wow. This was completely amazing, totally surprising and absolutely flattering. We sat down for wine and pasta, and he didn't leave my house after that for the next twelve years of our life and marriage.

I caught Peggy up on the romance as it flourished day to day. We were both happy about the presence of this kind and gentle man. She thought he was behaving correctly and was encouraged by my updates and reports.

Unfortunately, there were a couple of early warning signs I didn't pay attention to. A few months later, I invited him to go to Las Vegas with me while I was shooting a show. We had a gorgeous suite, complimentary room service and anything we could possibly want. While I was at rehearsal my *now* steady boyfriend went to the casino to play some Blackjack. Later that day as we were walking along the strip, he pulled the pockets of his jeans inside out and announced that he was dead broke. He said it with a tone of pride, almost gleeful at his pennilessness. It shocked me in the moment and I remember saying, "I sure hope this isn't a pattern because I want to be with a winner not a loser." My frank statement shocked him a little too. At the time I didn't pay attention to this but it became a "big deal" during our marriage. He thought his being "poor" was an acceptable thing, cute and darling even, and then he relied on me for financial support. It was an early warning sign I didn't heed.

Peggy knew things were rocky even before I did. She didn't like some of the things I told her he said to me and she certainly didn't like more of the things he did. I just thought it was *all my fault,* that I should be a better wife, or a better cook, or a better listener or a more open person, or more of *something* so he'd be happier. If he was happier certainly I would be happier and so it went.

Our marriage was pretty good for several years but unfortunately some of his old wanderlust tendencies began to surface. He felt he was getting old and wondered if he still "had it" when it came to women. I noticed him flirting at parties with pretty women, but when we discussed it, he always called it "networking." I trusted his words. Peggy didn't. She suspected he was "fooling around" long before I did. Then one day I asked her opinion and she told me she thought he was cheating. All the signs were there but I was the last to see them. It was all pretty typical. I blamed myself for not being enough. I felt I had to keep trying to make this work because I wanted to be happily married for 300 years like Peggy. She always seemed to be so happy. She had it all: a loving husband, three fabulous children, a career, a place in the community, national fame, best-selling books and a sunny smile that never quit. I wanted all of that too, so I thought I could-and should-emulate her life. She was my coach, my sounding board, my role model, my support system and my inspiration. What wasn't I doing right?

After months of introspection, and some help from my "Practitioner," Jerry, I acknowledged that there were other things as well that drove us apart. One of them was the vast cultural difference between us, especially surrounding his relationship with his mother and close relatives. In his culture family is very present, very interactive and come to stay for much longer visits that I was used to. And then there was my successful career which I believe was a bit overshadowing for him. We went to high profile parties and elegant social events. He was always *my* husband and *my* guest. He didn't have any events in his life that he could invite me to so he was always the invitee and not the inviter.

He did successfully reinvent himself during the course of our marriage and made an important career change. What I realized later in tallying up the lessons I had learned during this marriage was that I had forgotten to put on my 21-Day list of qualities for *The Love of My Life* that my mate value himself enough to be confident in generating his own success, mature with money and finances, and that he be capable of a lifelong, faithful relationship, no matter what he was experiencing inside. I needed him to be my friend, to be honest with me and to be someone I could trust completely. I was more than willing to be the same for him.

When my divorce was final I needed some time to recover from the blow. I went to see Jerry on a regular basis. Jerry is a Practitioner of Religious Science. He is a spiritual counselor and a transformer of lives so I decided to give myself some soul-nourishment from a spiritual perspective. Peggy was my dear friend and trusted advisor; Jerry was the professional. He brought perspective to me when I needed to see the big picture and stop fumbling around in my own feelings of self-pity. I got on with it. I healed with his help, then I went up to Peggy and Danny's house for a week and returned home with another adorable cat. To my delight, I realized that I didn't feel like a failure, nor did I belittle myself for not having had a long-term marriage. Instead, I celebrated myself for creating an almost-ideal mate, and I set out to find the next perfect *Love of My Life.*

I was fairly skilled at this 21-Day Process by now, so I did it again with even *more* precision and fervor. I had learned that I truly wanted a loving relationship, a whole and supportive, faithful partner, and a relationship that was mutual and reciprocal on every level. I was finished doing all the work and carrying the entire burden, be it emotional, financial or both.

I worked on specifics even more diligently this time. I was meticulous and detailed in every description. I even listed my love's favorite quotes and the precise notation of how he liked his hot dog. I was punctilious; I didn't leave one area undefined. At first I was worried that I was making it impossible for anyone to fulfill my "wish list." I even worried that my exacting specifications might limit my possibilities by not leaving enough room for surprise or spontaneity.

Was I ever wrong! By being specific and detailed I created a space in which the perfect person *could* show up. I'm so glad I didn't edit or correct my stream of consciousness thinking. The perfect person *did* show up, and it was a complete surprise for both of us. We fell in love easily with great compatibility. The rest of the "criteria" were already in place. We shared the same values, we lived in integrity, we shared spirituality, we loved to laugh, and we knew how to build mutual trust. We had both learned the "how tos" from past relationships and experiences. We each brought the gold we had mined from our accumulated life lessons into this new relationship and it sparkled in the sun.

Peggy had instructed me to, "Go back to church." She mentioned that she experienced me to be the happiest when I was actively involved in spiritual practices. "Hmmmmm" I thought to myself, "church, what a concept." Now, my church may not be your church, but I love it when I'm there. I practice Religious Science and have for 25 years. It's a metaphysical belief system that is non-denominational and encompasses all of the world's great teachings and master teachers. It accepts the teachings of Jesus, Buddha, Mohammed, the Dalai Lama, Mary Baker Eddy and all those who come from the pure source of Divine Creation. There is no exclusion, only inclusion, in this philosophy.

So, I drove down the hill to the nearest church of my choice, which just happened to be on the way to my dry cleaners (so it wouldn't be a total loss if I didn't like the church, I could always drop off my laundry and justify the trip!), and began to revitalize myself with these teachings. I enrolled in some classes and little by little began to get to know the minister.

Coincidentally, the minister was also single. As I became more active in the church, my exposure to the minister increased. We both loved to laugh and looked at the world as a humorous place. In a short time, we "clicked." We looked for ways to work on projects together because we had fun. The work I had done with the 21-Day Process began to take hold. Our values meshed, our hearts expanded when we were together, and we brought out the very best in each other. We spent as much time together as our lives and professions would allow. We discovered that we had a lot in common including a couple of mentors from our past. We were almost cut from the same cloth.

The nature of the situation required that we be discreet and really, really sure of our friendship and relationship before it was brought into the public eye. We were both extremely careful about the handling of it and were able to be very candid with each other concerning the impact of this relationship on the larger community. Dare I say it, but I was proud of how very mature and adult-like we were in our thinking and planning. Gradually, the congregation became aware that there was more to our relationship than merely

Minister-member. The beautiful point to all of this? Because our circumstances dictated we be *absolutely certain* of our relationship before we took bold steps in public, we went through all of the questions and answers together. Our relationship was mutually developed and we were able to create strong bonds before we ventured out into the world. Hence, there was nothing to be concerned about other than the mundane details of planning a life together. Our values were the same, our likes and dislikes similar and complementary. Even down to the geography (we lived the exact same distance from the church only in oppo-site directions), we were a perfect match. We are still that perfect match. And it feels so right and so good. Peggy and Danny are thrilled. (So is Jerry!) Finally! I got my perfect match. The key was finding the right person, not just *any* person, but the right one for me. Working through all of the questions and concerns ahead of time *with* the person was the piece that put our victory over the top. We did it and you can too.

What I want to convey to you about this process is that it works beyond the shadow of a doubt. You may find yourself doing what I did and perfecting this process across several relationships. You may need practice or you may nail it on the first attempt. If you stay completely honest with yourself, you will absolutely succeed. My greatest wish for you is that you work the process and see where it takes you. I promise the journey will be powerful, fun and exciting. You will create and revel in something you never would have called into your life before discovering these amazing 21 days.

CHAPTER THREE

More Success Stories!

I mentioned before that many of my friends watched me as I balanced myself on the acrobatic beam of romantic life. Sometimes I fell and ended up with a conspicuous bruise, other times I succeeded.

It was my successes they wanted to follow. After the second time I had attracted *The Love of My Life* a couple of my girlfriends wanted to know my secrets. I gave them a sketchy overview of what I did with the 21-Day Process, and they wanted to know more. So, I met with a group of them over coffee and explained the process in detail.

One of the women was a singer I met in a pre-recording session for a television special I was working on. She had a fabulous voice and a great wit. She and I had lunch together and bonded. For years we saw each other when she was in town. She wanted me to explain the process to her because she was living a life she didn't want to live and wanted to change it. Her fabulous voice had landed her many singing gigs with top recording artists but, she was always on the road traveling across country and flying internationally. (It seemed to be a glamorous life to the outsider. But she was tired of it). The glitz and glamour of the road wears thin after a decade of Holiday Inns and tour bus fumes. She was also tired of the social life on the road. After a day of travel, there was the concert to perform and she would sing and dance her little heart out. Then the band would retire to the local watering hole and there would be drinks and more drinks, some drugs, and always a few guys hitting on her. At closing time everyone went home with anyone they could and that was how it was on the road. Shallow.

It had become the nightly routine and the same old same old and she found no joy in it anymore. In fact, she had taken to going back to her hotel room, listening to music and reading a book after the concerts. The band teased and chided her for her convent-like life choice. They called her the "virgin singer" and tried to make her feel like a creep. While, they were out every night challenging their livers with hard whiskey, she was in her room having an apple.

Basically, she wanted to get off the road and do more studio work at home where she could create a stable life with a man she loved and possibly some children. She was leaving again to go on tour for the next three weeks, so it was a perfect time for her to experiment with the 21-Day Process.

She called me from the road to say she was enthralled with the work. It didn't matter to her anymore what the band thought or said. She simply did her job and then focused on writing her pages every night. One of the band members came over to her after a performance and asked her out. He knew she didn't want to be part of the rowdy bar scene, so he invited her to a local diner where they could just talk. It was a wonderful experience for her and, I believe, for him. They really connected over their chili and corn bread and got to know more about each other in one evening than they had for two years on the road. She wondered, "Was this process starting to work already?"

They had a few more evenings together and then his pregnant girlfriend showed up on the road to tell him about the "blessed event." She was sure he was even more disappointed than she was, and she could tell by the look in his eyes he was going to do the right thing even though it wasn't what he wanted in his heart. This incident gave her courage.

Finishing the 21 days was fun for her. She looked forward to the time alone and the opportunity for deep thought and almost prayerful wishing. Every night she made a ritual out of lighting a candle and sitting down at her desk on the road to write the description of *The Love of Her Life*.

She returned to Los Angeles, road-weary, and tired of eating fried food, but essentially pleased with herself for completing the 21 days.

Then an uncanny thing happened. She received a call from the lead singer she had been working with asking if she was free for a meeting. He had something he wanted to discuss with her. Well sure, it was "her boss" and all, so she absolutely, without hesitation, agreed to meet him for lunch the next day.

At the appointed time and location, he was waiting for her at a table in the back of a very "in" restaurant. They exchanged a few hellos and she smiled. He made small talk about the previous tour and asked her how she felt about being a member of the back-up singers. She told him she liked working for him, but she really loved the recording studio sessions the best. When she felt comfortable enough she shared with him her feelings about the stresses of the road and asked him how he felt about traveling so much of the time. He comfortably shared his private thoughts and the two of them spent the better part of the afternoon chatting and having a grand old time bonding. The restaurant workers began setting up for the evening service and asked if they would be staying for dinner. They both burst out laughing and the recording star said, "I am if you are!" She replied, "Yes, thank you, I will too."

What became evident to her was that this man had had eyes for her for a long time. His meeting with her was to announce that his divorce would be final in a few weeks and he was testing the waters to see if she might be interested in him as well. His wife had not traveled on the road with him and so the relationship had petered out after a time due to the separations caused by his line of work. The dinner lasted well into the early morning. They had an incredible time. The two of them had so much in common, so many experiences they could talk about and relate to, so many humorous recollections from the show and a deep respect for each other's incredible talents.

He was much more anxious to delve into a faster relationship with her because he enjoyed being married and having a partner and craved more companionship on the road. She was a little more cautious and took her time. Ultimately, a few months later they began living together, traveling together and living a mutually shared and complementary life. They married and she was able to have the children she wanted, (and he did too!), and although her home life was "the road," she was able to reconsider her priorities and adapt to life on the road with *The Love of Her Life.*

We laughed about the fact that he was already in her life big time, but until she did the work, and his life changed, nothing could happen. The timing was perfect and they remain happily married and taking their love and their children on the road. Even though she now travels in a private jet and has all kinds of help, she did the initial work by herself and she was just as surprised as anyone else about how it all turned out.

My second story is about a woman friend

who had been happily married and had a couple of children but had fallen on barren emotional soil with her husband. No matter what they said to each other, it was the wrong thing and set the other off.

Their early romance had been very sweet. He worked on one coast and she on the other. They "met in the middle" as often as they could and that ended up to be about once a month in Kansas. After a year of building up huge mileage accounts, they decided to move to the same coast, and it didn't matter which one. It was a fun few months while they each applied to different companies on both coasts. It was agreed that the best opportunity would be grasped because each was willing to make the move.

Much to their astonishment, both were offered jobs in the same city in the middle of the country. This time it was Cincinnati. They felt the Kismet and they soon were living and working in the same city, at new jobs and loving the synchronicity of the whole experience. Christmas time came and she was given a magnificent diamond ring as he popped the question. The answer was an immediate and heartfelt, "Yes." They were married six months later and bliss was written on each of their faces. I was invited to the wedding and happily attended.

For many years they lived a great life. Each had their own career and they created a couple of great kids and lived a tranquil life. Then her parents were taken ill simultaneously in another city and he was "downsized" from his executive position. She became not only the main breadwinner, but also the long-distance caregiver for her ailing folks and he sank deeper and deeper into depression. She was exhausted with her multiplying roles, and the kids continually asking, "Mommy why can't you come to my basketball game?" only further eroded her self-esteem and physical stamina. Her husband was trying to find a job, but as she did more, he retreated and shrank. They would have gone to couples counseling but she couldn't work it into her already overloaded agenda. And so, they became resentful and bitter towards each other.

Finally they decided to separate and figure things out before they did any real damage to their children with all the bickering and lack of respect each was dishing out to the other. The distance of separation seemed like a welcome vacation to both of them and they seized the idea with vigor.

He took an apartment in downtown Boston. She remained in their suburban home. They agreed to let ninety days pass without any communication except what was necessary in the exchange of children from one home to the other.

When I had dinner with my friend, I could see the pain and the fatigue in her eyes. She was drained. She felt conflicted; one day she felt relieved to be away from his barbed comments, and then the next she missed him terribly. She wanted to be the perfect wife, mother and daughter while being the perfect Vice President, too. It was a deep and burning anguish and she almost didn't know who she was anymore.

After listening to the many chapters of her saga, I suggested to her that she might want to try the 21-Day Process. At first she thought I was nuts. The last thing she needed was to attract another relationship into her life. She already had too many people in her life and they were all demanding her mind, body, soul, wallet and time. Together we figured out that this process, for her, might just be the clarifying one she needed to sort out her feelings, her priorities and the kind of life she wanted to lead.

So she did it. To this day I can't tell you how she managed to fit it in, but she did. She worked the 21-Day Process and at the end of it she felt much better about her life and her direction. She got clear in her mind and then described on paper the kind of relationship she wanted to have and the type of life she envisioned.

With her new clarity, having taken the time to think and probe deeply, she hired full-time caregivers to come into their home and care for her parents. She visited as often as she could. She then went on about the business of her life. At the end of the ninety days she faced the pre-ordained meeting with her husband. As she drove to the appointment, she had an uneasy feeling in her stomach and she was not sure this was an altogether good idea. He was waiting when she arrived. He had a big smile on his face because he was very happy to see her. They were careful and cautious with each other at first, and then the talk flowed more easily. He had pre-ordered her favorite wine and she was touched by the thoughtful gesture.

They laughed as they both said at the same time, "You first!" He told her he had been doing some substitute teaching at the local elementary schools. He loved it and he had quite a few endearing stories to tell her about this new adventure. She hadn't seen him this happy or this full of life in years. When the appropriate moment surfaced, she told him about the 21-Day Process. Initially his face darkened as she described its purpose. But he brightened completely when she told him of her own personal revelation. During the processes she realized the person she described as her perfect mate was *him!* It amazed her and was a bit disconcerting. But, as she continued the process, she understood more of what was happening. She *had* met *The Love of Her Life*, she just needed to refresh that page on her human browser. The night was a turning point for them. They had gone to the well and taken stock of themselves independently and yet returned to each other with a renewed vigor and a zest for life that created a 180-degree turn around.

Without the process she might never have realized the jewel she already had in her hands. And, without the time apart, he might never have found that his true mission in life was teaching. With new information they worked out the rest of the details and challenges of their life together. He was "off" in the afternoons so he could attend the children's events, and she was free to do what she needed to do and excel on the corporate plain. They brought the children into this creative way of handling life and everyone accepted it happily.

Eventually they each settled into more home-based careers. Her financial success allowed her/them to purchase a local magazine and she became the publisher she always dreamed of becoming. He went on to become a college professor and they now live a mutually respectful, blissful life in Kansas.

Yet another story, a male friend was a working buddy for years and years. He operated camera for the most popular TV shows and was on the "A" list. He was soft-spoken and never cracked under the pressure or the long hours of production. He always paid attention to his job and played by the rules. He was a calming influence in what could frequently be a raging storm.

When we were both young in the business he was always chasing something cute, tiny and vapid. Most of his dates giggled a lot and wanted to meet the stars of the TV shows he worked on.

One day, a new tenant moved into my apartment complex. She was a talented artist and photographer and eventually landed the job of photography editor for Playgirl Magazine. Her assignment was to find men to pose in the nude for the magazine layout. One particular night we had dinner, more than enough wine and laughed and laughed about various insane designs she might come up with for her business card. (How do you put in print what you actually "do" when its really asking men to take their clothes off and pose for you?) A few days later, she asked me, seriously, if I knew any cute guys that wouldn't mind posing for the magazine. First of all they'd have to come in for a photographic *audition* so she could see how they looked on camera. She was completely professional and deadly serious. I worked with a lot of men, so the next day at the studio I asked my friend the cameraman if he would be interested. Actually, I asked a few of the men and only my cameraman friend whispered, "Yes," as we were leaving for the day. So, I gave him my girlfriend's number.

The very next week he went in for the audition which turned out to be fun. Unfortunately he didn't make it into the magazine as Mr. September, but he did manage to get a few more dates with the Playgirl staff. A few years passed and he continued dating even thinner, younger and sillier women.

One day he was bursting with joy as he announced to me he was engaged and was running off to Vegas to get married. I was surprised because it seemed so sudden but he convinced me he was really in love this time and she was "different." I wished him well in case I didn't see him for another year. When I did see him, he looked a lot older. His hair was thinning and he was a bit stoop-shouldered. I knew better than to ask him how the marriage was working out. I could tell from the very sight of him the answer would be, "Not well."

"Oh dear," I said to myself, as I watched him slump into the booth at lunch. "What happened?" I asked. He just shook his head and berated himself for being so gullible and so stupid. The six-month marriage had cost him some money, but it also cost him some serious body damage, the paint job on his Porsche, and as his self esteem. It *seemed* as though they really did love each other. He mistook her interest in coming to the set to visit him for an expression of devotion. He didn't suspect his little sweetheart had bigger designs on her career than she did on him.

Basically, she considered him her footpath into showbiz and she marched her little white majorette boots right over the top of his prematurely balding head.

He couldn't believe it! He had been told for so many years he was "a good catch" and he had come to believe it as absolute truth. He was super shocked to discover she didn't share his belief. Had she been up front with him in the beginning and asked for his help, approached him honestly about her intentions, he would have gladly helped her achieve her dream of stardom. They might have had a beautiful marriage. But she didn't. The divorce was messy and he endured her selfish behavior throughout some painful legal finalizations. He faulted himself through it all. Even though she had taken a tire iron to his cherished vintage Porsche when she didn't get her way, he cut her slack. He was truly a great guy and it was obvious how much he was hurting. So I poked my nose a little further into his business and outlined for him the 21-Day Process. I noticed his eye twitch at the mere mention of a romantic relationship, but he listened politely and I left him with his own soul searching. Poor baby! I wanted him to be happy. He deserved it.

Another year passed before I saw him again. Show business is seasonal. When I did see him he it was raining but he was all sunshine. "Wow," I said, "what a transformation!" He gave me a "high five" and we dashed into the studio to get out of the rain. Over morning coffee we tried to speak, but stagehands were always interrupting and asking questions about where to put this or that completely ruining our social connection! Drat, it would have to wait for lunch! All morning long throughout rehearsal I kept thinking of his bright face and that big ole grin. At lunchtime I found out why.

I nearly dropped my chopsticks into my Pad Thai noodles when he told me he was not only seeing, but cohabitating with, a new love. He spoke in fast sentences as he described to me how he sat down a few months after our last lunch and worked the 21-Day Process. He was energized by it and started to look at his prospective dates differently. He didn't just jump at every pretty little thing that walked by. He was looking more deeply now.

Given the allure of his beachside residence, he was the prime target for relatives' visits. His third cousin had recently come out for a visit. She wanted to get into show business and asked to spend part of the summer investigating the possibilities. She agreed to pay utilities and help out with the housework; cooking and cleaning in exchange for a roof over her head. He said he liked coming home to someone. It was a new feeling for him. She was thoughtful and caring. She made him his favorite foods and left little notes that were sweet, gracious and genuine. She had met a young man and was seeing him a couple times a week. Occasionally the cousins would have dinner together, but never late nights because my friend always had very early morning studio calls. She took to getting up early and making him coffee and then went to the strand to exercise. They became great friends and one day as he was driving into work, he realized how much he was really was looking forward to seeing her that night. He called mid-day and she was happy to hear from him.

Shortly thereafter, he asked her out. Neither of them knew what to expect. They found they just enjoyed being together and having some fun experiences. He was re-discovering his city as he enthusiastically showed her the sights. She was delighted to have the attention. One night she talked deeply to him about her life. She confided to him things she had never told anyone else because she felt she could trust him. She had always had this special feeling and thought she was somehow different from the rest. One of the reasons she came to California was to explore the things that were restless inside. She told him she really liked women and was afraid to pursue a relationship, because what if she was wrong and how could she back track? What if her family found out and ostracized her? He forced himself to come to terms with his own feelings right on the spot. He told me later, how her candor and her sweetness had really touched him and how much he cared for her and her welfare. He reassured her that he loved her no matter what she discovered and he encouraged her to go out and see if she was right.

He introduced her to a gay woman he knew and she told his cousin about a few clubs she might like to "check out." My friend's disappointment lifted. He reported that initially he felt like an ocean wave had toppled him head first into the sand, only this time it was more humorous than it had ever been before. His Porsche was still intact as was his self-esteem, his manhood and his bank account. He was way ahead of the game and stronger.

The next paragraph might sound a little like stealing "Brokeback Mountain's" thunder. My friend confided to me he thought of joining a monastery because he was seemingly so unlucky in love until he went to his high school reunion. As you already may be thinking, this sounds too pat and too predictable, but he did have a great time at the reunion renewing old friendships. One of those was with his debate team partner. The two men had shared a couple of acting classes when they attended a liberal arts mid-western college. They had similar leanings when it came to show business. My friend went to Los Angeles and became a top-rated cameraman with no wife and no kids; the other went to New York and became a theatrical director *with* a wife and two kids. Over drinks and several conversations the two of them renewed their friendship. Before that friendship had been Platonic; now, things were taking an entirely different course. They became romantically involved and eventually developed a bi-coastal love affair.

My friend's mate didn't run out on his wife as you may think. For years they had an understanding. They remained best friends and co-parents living under the same roof while leading different social lives. Presently, my friend the cameraman and the New York director are on the same coast living together as a couple. The new relationship brought many wonderful elements together. They are both sharing "dad" duty to two lovely Asian-American children.

He credits the 21-Day Process for cleaning out the cobwebs and for encouraging deeper self-exploration. He wasn't totally prepared for the "switch" he experienced from a hetero-sexual to a homosexual lifestyle. But when it came so naturally, he found himself referring back to the 21-Day Process asking himself deeper questions. This exercise brought him new horizons and increased his romantic options. Instead of a wife, he got a husband. And, he is very happy.

I do not know what the 21-Day Process will do for you. It may change your entire life. Or it may just shift it a little. I am certain you will find a mate if you follow the program and stay the course.

I could tell you so many more stories, but it's time for you to create your own.

CHAPTER FOUR

Are You Ready, Willing and Able?

Before you begin the 21–Day process you will need to do a few things and purchase a few items.

To Do

If you are familiar with the process of meditation then meditate on the following questions. If you don't meditate, then choose a quiet location, carve out some personal time, search your soul and ask yourself the following questions. Be courageously honest with yourself. There are no *"wrong"* answers only responses that will clarify your feelings in preparation for the exciting process ahead.

Here are the questions:

- What do I expect from a relationship?
- Is there anything more important in my life than a relationship right now?
- What feelings do I get deep down when I think about having been in a relationship?
- Do I need more information or education about being in a relationship?
- What kind of baggage might I be carrying from past relationships?
- If I could picture my perfect life, what would it look like?
- Describe how you would feel if you were living your vision of this perfect life.

(The following pages are in journal form so you can fill them out as your answers come forth. Remember: be honest with yourself and as clear as possible with your answers.)

What do I expect from a relationship?

_____

_____

_____

_____

_____

_____

_____

_____

_____

_____

_____

*Is there anything more important in my life
than having a relationship right now?*

_____

_____

_____

_____

_____

_____

_____

_____

_____

_____

What feelings do I get deep down when I think about a relationship?

_____

_____

_____

_____

_____

_____

_____

_____

_____

_____

Do I need more information or education about being in a relationship?

_____

_____

_____

_____

_____

_____

_____

_____

_____

_____

What kind of baggage might I be carrying from past relationships?

_____

_____

_____

_____

_____

_____

_____

_____

_____

_____

If I could picture my perfect life, what would it look like?

_____

_____

_____

_____

_____

_____

_____

_____

_____

_____

Describe how you would feel if you were living your vision of this perfect life.

_____

_____

_____

_____

_____

_____

_____

_____

_____

_____

_____

It is important that you ask and honestly answer all of these questions. You might unknowingly be kidding yourself about your own expectations, so take the time to look within your own mind and heart to determine what you're really thinking and feeling. The more honest you are with yourself, the better the results you will achieve. You may want to use additional sheets of paper and expand your answers. Please don't shortchange yourself on this leg of the journey. You owe it to yourself and to your future partner to look deeply at these questions and candidly examine your answers. You may discover that this isn't the time for a relationship that will impact the rest of your life, or you may discover that you are truly ready in this instant. Whatever the outcome the answers are between you and your inner self. Do the work. Then move on to the next chapters in confidence!

Now, go shopping!

You will need to buy something special to write on or in. You may want to think about what that looks like after you've read a description of the process in the next chapter.

You can use something as simple as a legal pad, or as ornate as a gilded leather journal. You'll know exactly what you need and what fits your personal style. For the moment, just make a note that you'll need something to write on and something to write with.

If you're the casual sort, then the advertising pen you picked up from your neighborhood merchant will be fine, but if you're discriminating about your stationery products, you'll want to select and set aside a special pen. Just make sure it is comfortable, easy to write with, full of ink or gel and causes your hand no discomfort. You'll be using it a lot!

Read the next section for a description of the process, and then go shopping! (If you're anything like me, any opportunity to visit a stationery store is a cause for celebration!)

CHAPTER FIVE

How to Be Successful in Your Process

When you have really looked within and truly decided that you want a relationship, a partner, a true love, this process will flow from you like an ebullient stream. The very first partner you encounter in this process will be yourself. In the next 21 days you will not only become your own best friend, but your own coach, cheerleader and support system. It will happen automatically and without even thinking about it. Whether you choose to do this 21-Day Process alone or buddy-up with someone else who is seeking the same goal, it will still and ultimately boil down to *you-on-you*. No one else can create the *Love of Your Life* for you. If they did, it would be called an "arranged marriage." And none of us wants that, do we?

Here is an overview of your instructions/ agreements: Before you begin the process read the rest of this book. There is material that will guide and support you during the 21-Day Process in the succeeding chapters. Don't skip ahead without reading them.

Commit to 21 consecutive days. Block the time out on your calendar, palm pilot or day planner. Make it a standing meeting, appointment or date with yourself. The time of day can vary, but if your personality responds to order and you like precise organization, ink in the same time every day.

Set aside twenty to thirty uninterrupted minutes each day to do this process. Turn the phone off, turn *on* the answering machine, close down your computer, put the kids to bed or send them off to school and feed the cat or dog so they don't disturb you. This is *your* time. Plan for the twenty to thirty uninterrupted minutes and then take them.

Handwrite everything. No computers, word processors, or electronic devices are allowed. Your own hand must set these thoughts on paper. This is a key factor. Do not put anything between your mind, heart, pen and paper. Allow the answers to flow through your entire body onto the page. This is one of the key secrets of the process: be tactilely involved. This is imperative. No one will judge your penmanship; just write and write and write, the old-fashioned way.

Keep the agreement with yourself. Make no excuses; make no exceptions. This is serious work and you must take it seriously and honor it. You are creating your future and your happiness with this process. What else could be more important than that? If you find yourself continually breaking your agreements, you may not be really ready to make a commitment to finding *The Love of Your Life*. Are you being honest with yourself about wanting to love and be loved?

Agree to start all over again if you miss a day. It is critical to this process to keep your focus and build your pattern for 21 consecutive days. If you break the rhythm, you probably will not succeed with this process. So if you miss a day, go ahead and sigh, but move on to a new section in your writing pad and once again write, "Day 1". Begin again. (You'll get over your disappointment!)

Take No Breaks. The process is powerful if it is unbroken. If you become "stuck" or "frazzled" anywhere during the process, don't worry, it happens to everyone. We all experience temporary "blocks." If that happens for you, simply rest for a moment, don't fight the feeling. Be patient with yourself and the process. More will come and the writing will flow. Keep your pen in your hand and re-ask yourself the questions. Remember it is imperative that you write for at least twenty minutes and remain focused on your intention and your goal. (This is where self-coaching comes in. Refer to Chapter Eight on "Techniques.")

Begin on Day 1 according to your plan. If you enjoy music, put on a CD or strap on your i-Pod. Write "Day 1" on your page and read the affirmations for that day in Chapter Seven. *Now* you have officially begun to create the *Love of Your Life.*

Do Not Read or re-read anything you have written until the end of the 21 days. Allow each day to be unique and fresh or flat and redundant if it needs to be. It doesn't matter *what* you write, just *that* you write for twenty minutes each day. You may duplicate yourself.

That's just fine, remember, you aren't judging, grading or criticizing, you're just thinking out loud via your pen.

For twenty to thirty uninterrupted minutes a day, over 21 consecutive days, you will be handwriting everything that comes to mind. You are planting the seeds for your future. If you try to shortcut this process, you will shortcut your own life experience. This system has proven itself successful in many lives. Try not to outthink it, outguess it or improve upon it. You'll have plenty of time to do that later on if you wish. For now, just follow the plan as described if you want the results it offers.

My best friend Peggy, whom you met in Chapter Two, read all this and said, "Schwew! It sounds like a pretty tough list of things I'd have to do. If I were doing this, I don't know if I could do it all by myself. I might need a lot of help and encouragement along the way!" I always listen to Peggy. So there is help for you. You'll have what you need! In Chapter Seven you will find a day-by-day guide to follow as you continue in this 21-Day Process.

CHAPTER SIX

Working the 21-Day Process

With the music on, the door closed and your privacy assured, open your journal and pick up your pen.

You will be writing for the next twenty minutes so make sure you are *physically* comfortable.

There are a couple of ways you can approach these sessions. You can use your intuition and follow your own inner-direction to create the image of *The Love of Your Life*, or you can use the list of suggestions that follow. Always feel free to write extemporaneously and from your own heart. This is the best of the best because it comes from your own specialized and unique self.

If you prefer a little guidance in creating the description of *The Love of Your Life*, there are some jumping off points below. They can get you started and allow your creative juices to begin flowing. Feel free to depart from them at any time and let your own instincts take over, they are after all, the best guides you can call upon.

Fully describe each area and write until you can't possibly write anymore. Resist the urge to edit yourself and refrain from any judgment or opinion. Allow your self-expression to be uninhibited and playful. If you exceed the 30 minutes don't stop yourself, unless you have made another commitment which you really must keep.

Begin by going to Chapter Seven and reading the Affirmation for Day 1. Use the Affirmation to center yourself and set a positive tone for this exercise. As you begin to write out your descriptions longhand, describe *in as much detail as you can* the *Love of Your Life*. Repeat the process for Day 2 and so on. You can develop one or two points each day, or you can write about all of them at once. Just remember you have 21 days to write, so proceed at your own pace and be specific, meticulous and honest. (Refer to Chapters Seven and Eight if you find you need encouragement, inspiration or a prod.)

1. Describe his/her personality.
2. Describe his/her physical characteristics.
3. Describe the soul and character qualities he/she embodies .
4. Describe what he/she values most in life.
5. Describe his/her background (ethnic, education, life-experience).
6. Describe his/her childhood. (Make it up, it's part of the process.)
7. What makes him/her smile?
8. What is his/her favorite music?
9. What movies does he/she like?
10. If he/she had a day off from work, what would he/she do?
11. If he/she had five million dollars, describe what he/she would do.
12. Does he/she have a favorite color? If so, how does that show up in his/her life?
13. Is he/she a leader or a follower?
14. If he/she were a flower or a plant, what would that be?
15. If he/she played sports, what activity would that be?
16. If he/she had a secret, what would that be?
17. List the most important qualities that your Love has and describe why that is important to you.

18. Describe the five qualities that *The Love of Your Life* recognizes and appreciates in you.

19. Describe how you picture the year with *The Love of Your Life* playing out. Describe a birthday, Christmas, Valentine's Day, holidays, family gatherings, etc.

20. Describe his/her relationship with his/her mother.

21. Describe his/her relationship with his/her father.

22. Describe his/her relationship with other family members, if there are any.

23. Describe how this person emotionally supports you.

24. Describe your Love's financial situation.

25. Describe your sex life with this person.

26. Describe a day with this person from waking up through falling asleep.

27. What is his/her greatest fear?

28. What is his/her greatest love in life?

29. What makes him/her soar?

30. Why does he/she feel attracted to you and why does he/she choose you?

31. How does he/she like their hot dog? (What do they put on it?)

32. Add any further thoughts of your own.

Twenty to thirty minutes can seem like a very long or a short time; it's all relative, like waiting at a stoplight when you're in a hurry or holding your hand over a flame. Who's to say but you, how long a minute really is? What you make of this time will be the most important factor.

Do only as much as you can. This should be a joyous exercise not a prison sentence. Try not to exceed one hour, even if you have a lot to say. Set a timer if you need to. There will be other days and times-tomorrow as a matter of fact.

Let your thoughts, impressions, images and ideas flow. And please, resist any tendency you have to correct or second-guess yourself. Don't even bother correcting the spelling or the grammar at this stage, just let the truth and the descriptions cascade from deep within you. Resist the urge to be a "critic" and just let the process emanate from your heart.

You can ask these same questions every day and respond to them on paper, or you can ask one or two a day. You can also toss them all aside and invent your own questions, or follow your own spontaneous train of thought. The essential two elements are daily time (twenty to thirty minutes) and 21 consecutive days of writing down your personal stream of consciousness as it relates to and defines *The Love of Your Life.* You have everything to gain.

CHAPTER SEVEN

Affirmations and Coaching for Your 21-Day Process

You may find by beginning with an Affirmation before you start your daily writing you will be more centered and focused on the task at hand. You can use the Affirmations in this chapter consecutively, as they are listed, or you can vary the list and use the ones that speak to you and your feelings that day. Writing down a phrase or a statement as opposed to saying it has historically been a proven method for surefire success. Your feelings may change considerably from day to day, after all you are dealing with deep emotional material. You may want to write the Affirmation at the top of your page before you begin each session. It is your choice.

Do what feels right for you. Refer back to the Affirmation of the day during your writing process if you need help to remain focused or stay on target.

Day 1:   *I am capable of doing anything I choose. Nothing and no one stands in my way, not even me.*

Feelings: On this day you may be filled with excitement, great joy and anticipation. You may want to plunge right in and get it all done. Remember, San Francisco wasn't built in a day, and the best way to create a solid structure is one stone at a time. You will have plenty of time to write. You have another 20 days ahead of you. Start gently, stay centered and write from your deepest feelings.

Day 2:   *I possess all of the natural qualities, gifts and talents I need to accomplish any goal I set my mind and heart to.*

Feelings: Today you may feel as excited as you were yesterday. You have a whole day under your belt and you are feeling good. Am I right? You have some confidence built up in yourself and this process. You can't wait to see some results. Good! Keep that energy, continue to write as honestly as you can, and then let it all go. You're doing great. Keep up the good work.

Day 3:   *Something is changing within me and I can see and feel the positive change.*

Feelings: Did someone smile at you today? Did you get a glimpse of what is in store for you as you continue to open your mind and heart? Are you feeling a little bit better about your place in this universe as a happy, partnered, successful-in-love kind of person? Or did somebody cut you off on the freeway and in retrospect you realize that you vented your insecurities on them? No matter what happened, put it all aside and start anew. You're doing just fine. Keep going!

Day 4: *I am worthy of love. I extend my love and it is given back to me tenfold. I like myself and who I am. Others delight in being with me.*

Feelings: Renewal is the word for today. Open your new page and approach your work on this process as a breath of fresh air. Write what you think and feel, and use the questions from the list that invigorate your heart. Be careful not to overthink anything at this point. Just keep the writing flowing and let it out.

Day 5: *Everyone enjoys being around me because I spread joy and exude love.*

Feelings: Now you're into a pattern. You

know what to expect. You may be facing the process as a "job" or you may be experiencing the excitement building each day. Good news! Whatever you do, don't fret! Keep going. Stay focused on your goal.

Day 6: *I am a beautiful person inside and out and I receive compliments and praise easily and with grace.*

Feelings: You may be starting to experience a sense of repetition now. You might even feel like there's no light at the end of this tunnel. Or, you are jazzed and excited by this process. Maybe a little bit of both creeps into your awareness. You can always go back to earlier questions and answer them again. There is no such thing as a hard and fast rule with this process. Be creative and use it according to how you are feeling. Continue writing.

Day 7: *Love is pouring into my life from all directions.*

Feelings: Congratulations! You have completed one full week. You are one-third of the way to *The Love of Your Life*. You deserve a giant pat on the back. So give yourself one and then finish your writing for the day. Treat yourself to something very special today. You have earned it!

Day 8: *I magnetize love and affection with every action I take, in everything I say and wherever I go.*

Feelings: Maybe this is the day you are tired. Perhaps you awoke feeling like it's all too much. Maybe you didn't. Maybe you were totally energized and ready to face the day. No matter what your physical or mental state, focus your intention on the *Love of Your Life*. Be willing to put your feelings and your emotions aside and do the necessary work. Sit down, relax and write. Even if you lose focus now and then, do your best to remain centered. Discipline may be required. Do what you can, write from your heart and it will be just fine.

Day 9: *I am in love and I am loving.*

Feelings: You are beginning the next phase of this process. By now you may be experiencing personal enlightenment on a very deep level. With all that's going on inside, you may be finding it difficult to fill the page, or, you may be getting writer's cramp from all that you have to say. Remember, it's only 21(short) days out of your life to create the future of your dreams. You're worth it!

Day 10: *Love comes to me easily and effortlessly.*

Feelings: Even if past relationships have not been easy, try to entertain the possibility that your new relationship will be. It can be filled with joy, mutual respect and gentleness. It can be wild, exciting, gentle and tender all at the same time. Don't waver. Keep your thoughts on the end goal. Feelings may arise that surprise you. Remember, you are delving deeper than you ever have before and feelings are bound to emerge. Trust the process and keep writing.

Day 11: *I am enjoying my new relationship. I have fallen in love with myself and everyone else.*

Feelings: No matter what is going on today, you are creating your new Love with every stroke of your pen. You are claiming what you want in your life and you are being very specific so it can come to you. If your mind drifts, or you are feeling impatient, or you think this is all just a silly waste of time, remember your goal. Hang in there. It's a short process when you really think about it. It will be over in three weeks if you stick to the plan. Recommit to your end goals and you will find a new energy arising to move you through the process.

Day 12:   *The Love of My Life is seeking me with the same intensity as I am seeking him/her.*

Feelings: Oh sure, some days it doesn't "feel" like any of this is true at all. Some days it feels like the ship has left the dock, the train has pulled out of the station, and you weren't on it. Have faith! There's always another ship that will come in or another train you can catch. Like clockwork, they come and go. You *will* get there. Just buy your ticket and stand in line a little longer and you'll be on your way. Don't give up now. Hang in there. Picture your destination, take a moment to feel what it's like to have arrived and then pick up that pen and go, go, go!

Day 13: *This 21-Day Process is a winner for me, and I succeed in attracting The Love of My Life to me.*

Feelings: You are almost ready to cross a major milestone. If you're having doubts, think of your love-filled future. Think five years from now and picture how you are celebrating your anniversary. Don't let go of that image. Refocus your energies and create that perfect mate and your ideal relationship. Dig deeper for even more truth than you thought you could. Be the bravest and the most courageous person you know. You can do it. Keep writing.

Day 14:   *My heart is full and brimming over. I grow in self-honesty every day. I love the trust I am experiencing.*

Feelings: Hurray! You're at the two-thirds mark. You have only more week to go. One week only! Don't worry, you'll make it! You've still got a lot more to say. Don't be concerned if you start to repeat yourself. Remember, your job is to write your thoughts and feelings down. This is not an essay contest; you will not be graded on it. Just let your feelings flow and capture them on paper.

Day 15:   *The Love of My Life is no longer a distant dream.*

Feelings: Today, listen to your inner voice. Find the stillness within you and really allow that silent wisdom to have a voice. You may be surprised at how much will be revealed. You know the phrase,

"Out of the mouths of babes"? Let this be out of the mouth of the young innocent voice within you. Take your time, allow it to emerge and you will learn so much more about love in your life. Today listen deeply to your heart and keep writing.

Day 16:   *He/she is real in my life.*

Feelings: Today is a turning point. It is the day when you begin to genuinly feel the presence of love within you and in your life. Doubts may arise throughout this process. It is natural for them to surface. Those doubts allow you to ask deeper questions and to search for more authentic answers. If a doubt arises, just know it is there for a purpose. It is reminding you to pay more attention to something. Is that a question about your own worthiness to be loved? Is it caution surfacing about making a lifelong commitment? What else could this doubt be telling you? Don't give the doubt any more power than that of a question. Answer the question clearly and then dismiss it.

Day 17: *I am comfortable, I am at ease and I allow all possibilities to flow through me.*

Feelings: A river is constantly flowing, constantly moving. You can never step into the same river twice because by the time you do, the water you first stepped into has passed and the river has changed. If you could live your life like the river, you would flow with the changes in the current and the intensity of the water, and adapt to each surge and swell without resistance. You would be in complete harmony with nature. See how you can use today's work to be like the river. Just flow with what comes from the stream of your own consciousness and offer no resistance. Be the river and just write.

Day 18: *I am The Love of his/her Life.*

Feelings: Today you are stepping up to the plate. You have reached the place where you claim your birthright to happiness. You are declaring that there is a perfect match for you somewhere in the world, and that you are absolutely entitled to have that someone love you, cherish you and choose to be with you. You know it is real in the pit of your stomach. Even if your knees shake a little when you make the statement, say it anyway. Believe it because it is the truth. Write from a very deep and honest place. Stay strong in your belief and your resolve. Say it, feel it and claim *The Love of Your Life.*

Day 19: *Everything I need is already inside of me.*

Feelings: Feeling like you are coming in for a landing? It's time to get excited about your final approach! You've done the work. You have put in long hours. You have opened your mind and heart to new thoughts and concepts. You have looked at many of your beliefs and your values, and you've probably made some inner shifts. You've had good days and not so good days. You've shed tons of new light on different aspects of your thinking about relationships. You have been fearless in your commitment to telling the truth. You've done all that, and more, haven't you? Take a nice deep breath. You're almost there. Stay centered on what you truly want. Let your nervousness subside and get out your pen. Keep writing.

Day 20: *I believe, I know and I accept that I am Love Itself, walking and talking as me and through me.*

Feelings: Today you take responsibility for being the love that you seek. As you write today, reflect on how Love shows up in your everyday life. The ultimate goal is to love and be loved with the same reciprocal intensity. The demonstration of love does not have to be identical, but the partner you are attracting brings loving equality into the relationship. Be very specific today about what that equality looks and feels like for you. Successful partnerships are made from two whole and complete beings, each bringing his/her own gifts and talents to the relationship in equal measure. Write about the balance and keep that in mind as you take up your pen in the second to the last day of your courageous process.

Day 21: *I release any fears I may have had in the past. I am renewed and I am free. I accept The Love of My Life right here and right now.*

Feelings: Love is in the air! You are at the last step of your process. Do you feel the victory welling up inside you? What a feat you have accomplished. Bravo to you! It took great courage and ardent discipline to reach this point. Now, you are only a few minutes away from completing the process. Wheeeeee!

Go ahead. Pick up that pen for the very last time. Let the writing flow as you put the final touches and your concluding thoughts on paper. Write from your heart. Write as if the relationship is already here and you hold it in your hands. Write from the place of conviction. Consider it a "done deal," and let it burst forth from you into your journal.

Day 22:

"Day 22? What are you talking about? I thought this was a 21-Day Process!" you challenge!" Well yes it is. It is a 21-Day Process. But on the 22nd day you have just one more tiny thing to do. Burn the pages. That's right. Burn them! Find a method that is safe and sane, and light them on fire. Cinder-city! This action releases your intention, your statements, your thoughts and all of your work into the universal energy that receives them and immediately puts *them* to work for you. As you light the pages on fire, say the following concluding affirmation:

I am secure and happy with the work I have done.

I now know I am pure love, and I attract the perfect Love of My Life. *I am attracting Love at this very moment. I release the complete body of my thoughts into the Universe so it may return to me exactly what I have described and claimed for myself, right here and right now. I believe it, I accept it and it is done!*

Now you have completed the process!

CHAPTER EIGHT

Techniques to Help You Manage the 21-Day Process

During the 21-Day Process you will be experiencing the natural ebb and flow of life and its challenges. One day you might feel bored, another day you may be exhausted, yet another day you might be on top of your game and raring to go. Whatever the situation is, you may need a little help to get through all 21 days. Read through these suggestions so that you can "push" yourself just a little bit if you have a day when you think you want to quit, postpone or give up. Remember, if you don't do the 21 days consecutively, you have to begin again!

Self-Coaching

* There are pages at the end of this chapter that you can use for the notes to yourself.

- Be sure to write down your "goals" for doing this 21-Day Process before you begin.
- For extra emotional support take time to create a mission statement for yourself as if you were a company and needed a reason to exist. Say it in twenty-five words or less and write it down.
- Collect or write down any inspiring quotes, sentences or sayings that motivate you and give you courage to go on. It could be as simple as "Go For It" or as complex as Dr. Martin Luther King's, "I Have a Dream" speech.

Cheerleading

- Write down the phrases that your teammates might say to you if you were playing in a team competition of some sort. List some "rah-rah" phrases that amuse and delight you and get you moving. (Personally I like, "Yeehaw!")

Support

- Call your best friend and ask him/her to speak a few phrases of support, or just remember what they have said to you in the past that made you feel better about yourself when you were taking positive action or following a dream. Make a list you can refer to frequently as you need it.

Even Deeper Support

Here are a few additional things you can do to deepen your commitment and enhance your experience of the process.

Meditation

If you are not in the habit of meditating, then just find a quiet spot, close your eyes, and follow the internal movement of your breath. As you begin to relax fill your mind with the statements and affirmations in the previous chapter, or simply focus on how you truly see yourself experiencing *The Love of Your Life*. Let those thoughts engulf you for a few minutes. Try this several times a day until you are comfortable with stillness and until you can really feel how this process clears and focuses your intention and actions.

If you are an experienced meditator, use the following suggested phrases or those in Chapter Seven to focus on as you begin your meditation.

- I am a powerful magnet. I see and feel how perfectly and easily I draw to myself *The Love of My Life.*
- I am a whole, complete and desirable being just as I am right here and right now; *The Love of My Life* is a whole, perfect and complete being just as he/she is right now. We are attracting each other at the same rate and with the exact same intensity right now. I accept that perfect truth.
- *The Love of My Life* is seeking me just as consciously and vigorously as I am seeking him/her. I accept that as the complete and total truth.
- My actions are complete and my intentions are crystal clear. I accept into my life *The Love of My Life* and our wonderful relationship. I am open, willing and able to accept this amazing gift.

Magnetism

Create a field of energy around yourself by simply closing your eyes and visualizing yourself as a magnet. Take a moment and imagine a magnet at work, or go on to the Internet to a science page or click onto this site: *http:// www.fhsu.edu/te/facstaff/gtaggart/lessons/fall 01/magnets3.html* to learn how magnets scientifically work. Then, take a moment (or two or three) to see yourself *as* that magnet. Let yourself feel the pull *as* the magnet and as you attract items to you. Once you have mastered the feeling of *you as the magnet* then change the objects you are attracting from "things" to "people" and see them magnetized to you in your imagination.

Attraction vs Attractive

If you look up Webster's definitions you find, *Attraction:* "the act of drawing to; the force which draws together bodies or particles; the affinity existing between one chemical body and another;" *Attractive*: "to cause to approach; to allure; to provoke notice."

There is an unseen force in the Universe called "attraction." Think of it as a verb. Take a moment to write down, or just think about how you might consider the words "attraction" and "attractive" to be different and then consider the meanings you have attached to them. Think of "attractive" as if it were a noun, a quality and not an action word. It is easy to intertwine and confuse the two ideas. Separating them and clearly understanding their differences is a key to attracting *The Love of Your Life.*

Do you think you have to be more attractive (adjective) to be *"attractive"* (verb)?

Attraction has nothing to do with being attractive. It is an unseen, invisible force in the universe that is part of natural law. It is deeper than the ocean and older than dirt. You will do well in love if you concentrate your thoughts and your inner energies on your powers, your qualities and your methods of attraction.

If you feel you could be more attractive in the physical sense, then go take care of that as well. Lose the weight, get a cosmetic makeover, try out a new hair color or a new hairstyle, buy some new clothes or do something that makes you feel like a million bucks and really positive about your appearance.

But whatever you do, don't confuse attraction and attractive any longer.

Staking a Claim

When we speak in the present tense and make a statement as if it were true, we call this "claiming." The statements in Chapter Seven are "claims" or affirmations. It's easy to learn and is one of the quickest ways for you to receive your stated desires. There is no guesswork in the process, so be clear and make all statements in the present tense and use positive words. Here are some examples:

- I claim *The Love of My Life* for myself. I have expressed my intentions clearly and I am deserving of a loving, fulfilling relationship. It is my right as a loveable human being to have the relationship I have stated and in this moment here and now, I claim that relationship as my own.
- I declare in this moment that I am worthy of happiness, love and a fulfilling relationship. I am a loving and love-worthy human being and I claim this as my right. I allow myself to accept it openly, willingly and gratefully.
- I see *The Love of My Life* right here and right now. He/she is present and we are enjoying the fruits of a loving and

fulfilling relationship. I am complete in this moment and in this partnership. I am filled with joy and overflowing with genuine love and appreciation. We are together and it is so good.

- I experience good in everyone and in everything I encounter. My life is working beautifully and the world supports me in all I do. I give out and receive love easily. I am a magnet for happiness and joy.

Self-Coaching

My goal for the 21-Day Process is:

_____

_____

_____

_____

_____

_____

_____

_____

_____

_____

My mission statement for this 21-Day Process is:

_____

_____

_____

_____

_____

_____

_____

_____

_____

_____

My inspirations are:

_____

_____

_____

_____

_____

_____

_____

_____

_____

_____

_____

_____

_____

_____

_____

_____

_____

_____

_____

_____

_____

_____

Positive things my ideal teammates would say to me:

_____

_____

_____

_____

_____

_____

_____

_____

_____

_____

Phrases my best friend would say to me for encouragement:

_____

_____

_____

_____

_____

_____

_____

_____

_____

Special Notes to myself:

_____

_____

_____

_____

_____

_____

_____

_____

_____

_____

_____

_____

CHAPTER NINE

Turning 21

It's a blessing that we all have different paths and march to the beat of a different drummer. Can you imagine a world of clones? Boring beyond belief! Your path should be and will be different and unique to you. There is no way to predict the details of the outcome; only you can do that. I can only testify that the 21-Day Process has worked for me and for many of my friends. Practice makes perfect. Feel free to throw out the things that don't work or that feel forced or uncomfortable for you, and embrace wholeheartedly the ones that do work.

Be sure to stay completely honest with yourself. Don't fall into the trap of saying or claiming anything other than what comes directly from your heart. Avoid, at all costs, repeating self-defeating words of messages you heard in the past. Don't write anything that isn't truly and honestly your own idea. Other people have great ideas about what we should be doing and thinking, cast those aside and write down only what *you* want.

Really listen to what is being said to you: note the tone of voice, an accentuated word, or what is left unsaid. Don't jump in before you know the temperature of the water. People tell us things about themselves all the time. We get into trouble only when we don't listen to what they are *really* saying and we focus instead on what we *want* to hear. We often get into an unwanted situation because we didn't pay attention to the indicators.

Peggy is my best friend and my support system. Sometimes it was hard hearing what she had to tell me, but I knew she was always honest and had only my welfare in mind. Be sure, when you pick your advisor or group of advisors that you select people you respect and trust. Even if you don't like what your advisor or advisors may have to say, listen. You selected them for their honesty, now close your mouth and hear them out. They are there for *you*. They love you. They possess the perspective that you may lack in the moment. They care about you. Consider for a moment how hard it is for *them* to tell *you* something you don't want to hear. They want everything to be wonderful for you, and if they are truly your friend and support system, they'll tell you the truth even if it's messy. So listen lovingly and don't make it harder for them. In the long run, it will turn out better for you that you did. And seek professionals when you need extra help. Counselors and spiritual advisors can help you enormously when you are working on specific goals.

Some people are meant to be *Mr. or Ms. Right Now*. Allow that possibility when you are dating. If they truly are to be *The Love of Your Life* and create a lasting relationship with you, it will happen. If they are only temporary and here as a teacher for you, then let that evolve and be ready to gracefully move on. The key to maintaining your sanity throughout this process is to find ways to be grateful for the gifts each person brings to you and then to move into the next phase without blame, resentment, anger or bitterness. See each as a messenger of good, and be grateful for the lessons. Avoid cynicism and blame.

Be aware of the early warning signs. If someone exhibits a behavior you know you don't want in your life, or if he or she tells you something you don't like, pay attention. The sooner you pay attention to these warning signs, the sooner you can move on to your perfect love. Listen carefully to the way you are spoken to and spoken about. Be sure you like what you hear.

Enjoy the process. This is a wonderful and fun time for you. Take delight in the events as they unfold. Bask in the attention you are getting. Take your time and don't rush to completion. A great deal of the fun in romance is the chase. Allow yourself to experience the joy and delight of these times. There will be many hours in the future when you'll look back with fondness on this period of your life. Grant it the latitude to enrich you and create lasting memories.

Know the difference between Lust and Love. Many people confuse one with the other; after the Lust wears off, they have very little energy left for the Love. Learn more about yourself and your "animal instincts" and be able to discern which is which in a given situation. Ask yourself: "If there were no physical relationship with this person, would I still be able to love him/her, be with him/her, cherish him/her, talk intimately with him/her?" If the answer is "No" then separate from those feelings (attraction) and move on. Imitate the bee's relationship to a flower. Get the nectar you need and then move on to another flower. The garden is filled with flowers; make sure you settle on the one that nourishes you the most, not just the one with the prettiest blossom.

Once you begin attracting people to you, stay conscious! Keep evaluating. Be honest with yourself about everything. *Everything!*

Remember to have a great deal of fun with this process. Take it seriously and do the work, but don't take it *too* seriously; it's not brain surgery. It is a natural, ebbing and flowing process, and you will succeed. You absolutely will!

If you need more advice or encouragement, I can be reached at *http://www.spiritualge nius.com.* You can E-mail me your questions and feedback anytime. I will respond and I'm also available for private counseling, tutoring or cheerleading. Pompoms included.

More than anything else, I want more love, more joy and more romance for this world we live in. I want *you* to find that love and bask in your birthright to love and be loved.

If you do that, you've made the world a better place for me, for you, and for anyone else who believes in and knows the power of love.

So, go out and find *The Love of Your Life*. (And if you already have one, go over and hug that person and celebrate your special love!)

Remember what the Italians say:

Volere e Portere

(Where there's a will, there's a way!)

Private Consultation is Available.

If you are truly serious about wanting a spiritually fulfilled life you can absolutely have it. You possess all the tools you need in the preceding fifteen chapters to personally achieve that result.

It takes work. It requires dedication and a fair amount of discipline. They key point to remember is to keep the fun in it. None of the work is arduous. Every step includes great joy and can be achieved through humor and practice. And, you can always book a private session with the author for more in-depth and personal assistance. Log onto www.spiritualgenius.com for details.

More Books From Dr. kac young

Discover Your Spiritual Genius

A compendium of helpful shortcuts for your spiritual development. This is the beginner's guide to knowing it all. You need this book if you're feeling down in the dumps or if your life isn't working they way you want it to. If you read and follow this advice life will take on a new meaning, you will be on top of your game, in charge of your life, happier, and more fulfilled.

Feng Shui, the Easy Way

The ancient art that can change your life overnight. This is a shortcut to proven Feng Shui principles and practices which can create immediate results in your life.

Dancing With the Moon

Learn how to use the natural energies of the lunar forces to orchestrate your life, your emotions and to create a deeper experience of living life at its fullest measure. Dancing With the Moon is easy to learn and simple to use. You will be enriched daily with this process.

Star Power

Create the year you want and fulfill your dreams by working with the energies of the stars and the planets. You can create the life you have always wanted by following these 12 simple steps to harness the cosmic energies that are just out there waiting for you.

Runes for Women
A Divination Tool for Today's Goddess

An ancient divination technique that reveals and utilizes the secrets of many powerful cultures. This book changes the entire perspective on the Runes and brings out the original Goddess quality of the Runic oracle.

....

You might also enjoy reading, *How to Marry the Man of Your Choice* by Margaret Kent if you want more ideas on finding and selecting a mate. ISBN: 0-446-69279-4

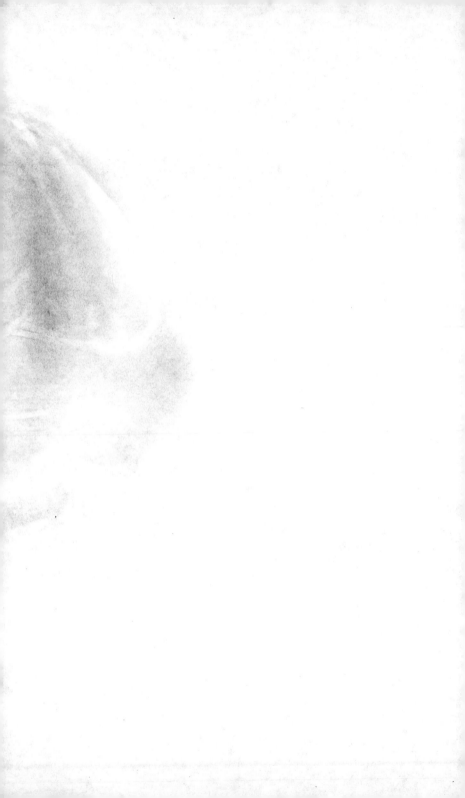